T0040608

3 Beloved Tales

Rapunzel

stories around the World

by Cari Meister

PICTURE WINDOW BOOKS
a capstone imprint

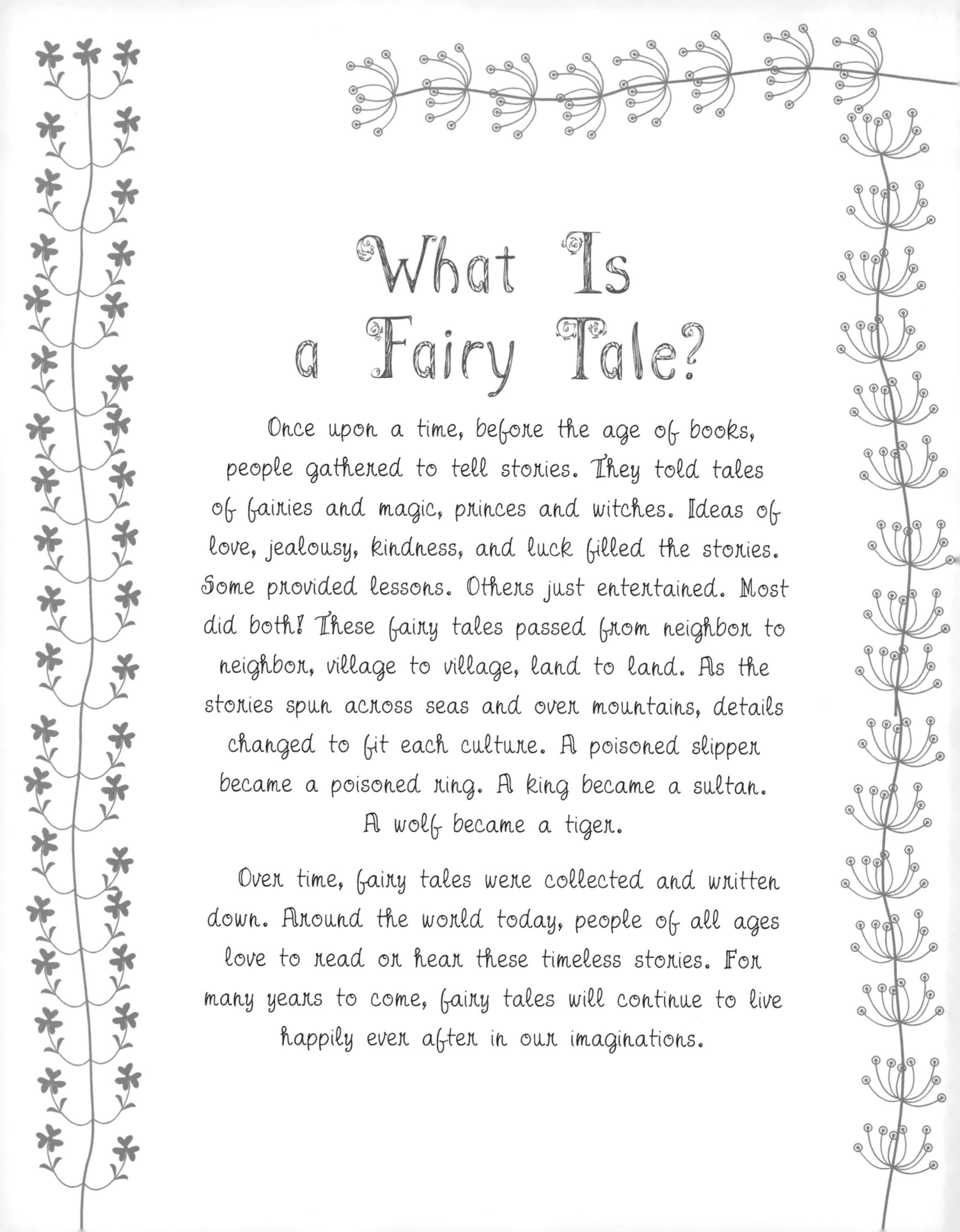

What Is a Fairy Tale?

Once upon a time, before the age of books, people gathered to tell stories. They told tales of fairies and magic, princes and witches. Ideas of love, jealousy, kindness, and luck filled the stories. Some provided lessons. Others just entertained. Most did both! These fairy tales passed from neighbor to neighbor, village to village, land to land. As the stories spun across seas and over mountains, details changed to fit each culture. A poisoned slipper became a poisoned ring. A king became a sultan. A wolf became a tiger.

Over time, fairy tales were collected and written down. Around the world today, people of all ages love to read or hear these timeless stories. For many years to come, fairy tales will continue to live happily ever after in our imaginations.

Rapunzel

illustrated by Valentina Belloni

A German Fairy Tale

Once upon a time, there lived a man and a woman who desperately wanted to have a baby. Year after year they waited. No baby came.

The couple lived next to a sorceress who had a magnificent garden. One day the woman noticed a bed of rapunzel. It looked so delicious. She longed for it more than anything.

"If I don't have that rapunzel," the woman told her husband, "I will die."

So the man climbed over the garden wall and stole a handful for her. Oh, how fresh and crunchy it tasted! His wife was content that night.

The next day, she asked for more.

Again the husband climbed over the wall. This time the sorceress was waiting.

"How dare you steal from me!" she yelled. "You will pay for this!"

"Be merciful," the man begged. "My wife saw your rapunzel and was overcome with longing for it."

"Very well," the sorceress said. "Take the rapunzel, but under one condition: I will take your first child in return."

The man, not knowing what else to do, agreed.

In time the woman gave birth to a baby girl. True to the agreement, the sorceress took the child. She named her Rapunzel and locked her in a tall tower near the forest. The tower had only a small window at the top.

Rapunzel grew into a beautiful woman with long golden hair. Whenever the sorceress wanted to see her, she would call, "Rapunzel, Rapunzel, let down your hair!"

Rapunzel would lean out the window and let her hair fall to the ground. Up the sorceress would climb.

One day a prince was riding through the forest. He heard Rapunzel singing. The prince wanted to see her, but there was no way into the tower.

The next day the prince returned. He hid behind a tree and watched as the sorceress called out and climbed up Rapunzel's hair.

After the sorceress left, the prince tried. "Rapunzel, Rapunzel, let down your hair!" he said. The golden hair appeared, and up the prince climbed.

The prince instantly fell in love. When he asked Rapunzel to marry him, she agreed. But she had no way out of the tower.

"Each time you visit," she said, "bring some silk. I will tie it together to make a rope."

So little by little, the silk rope grew.

Soon the sorceress found out about the prince. Furious, she cut off Rapunzel's hair and cast her deep into the woods. Then she waited in the tower for the prince.

When the prince called, "Rapunzel, Rapunzel, let down your hair," the sorceress let down Rapunzel's hair. When the prince reached the window, the sorceress cackled.

"You will never find Rapunzel!" she squawked. "She's gone forever!"

Full of sadness the prince leaped, landing on a thorn bush that poked out his eyes. The prince wandered the woods, blind and heartbroken, for many years.

Then one day he heard singing. Rapunzel! Upon seeing her prince, Rapunzel cried. Her tears fell into his eyes, and his sight returned. Rapunzel and the prince found their way back to his kingdom, where they lived happily ever after.

Clotilde

illustrated by Eva Montanari

A Filipino Fairy Tale

Long ago in a distant land, there lived a king named Ludovico. Ludovico was friends with a magician who was deeply in love with Ludovico's daughter, Clotilde. But beautiful Clotilde was not interested in the old magician.

Spurned, the magician turned bitter. Before he died he locked Clotilde, three magical horses, and two magical necklaces in a tall tower.

Ludovico was deeply saddened. He offered money, his daughter's hand in marriage, and the kingdom itself to any man who could set his daughter free.

Hundreds of men—princes and peasants—tried. All failed. The tower was simply too tall.

At last a man named Juan arrived. Both of Juan's brothers had tried to climb the tower and failed. They told Juan not to try. His parents also told him not to try. "You will shame us if you fail," they said.

But Juan was strong-willed. He was also kind-hearted, clever, and very good-looking.

Juan gathered nails, a long rope, and a hammer. He drove the nails into the tower. Then he tied the rope to the nails. After several days he made a rope ladder that reached all the way to Clotilde's window.

When Clotilde and Juan saw each other, they fell instantly in love.

"Please, take one of my necklaces as a sign of my love," she said.

But before Juan could thank her, his rope ladder began to give way.

Juan's jealous brother had pulled out all the nails!

"I shall fall to my death!" Juan cried.

Clotilde quickly called to one of the magical horses. She told Juan to jump on, and he did.

Unfortunately, Juan had no way of controlling the horse. It dropped him in a strange country far, far away. There he wandered, lost and hungry.

Many years passed before Juan found his way home. He wanted to see Clotilde, but he guessed that she was already happily married to someone else.

Heartbroken, Juan found work with a kind old man named Telesforo.

Meanwhile, King Ludovico had made another proclamation: Whoever could match his daughter's necklace could marry her. Many tried to copy Clotilde's necklace, but all failed.

News of the proclamation reached Juan. He wrapped up the necklace Clotilde had given him and asked Telesforo to bring it to the palace.

When Clotilde saw the necklace, she gasped. She knew it was the one she had given Juan. Telesforo told her that Juan was alive. Clotilde was filled with joy.

Shortly thereafter Clotilde and Juan were married. King Juan and Queen Clotilde lived to old age, ruling their lands in peace and happiness.

Petrosinella

An Italian Fairy Tale

illustrated by Colleen Madden

Once upon a time in Italy, there lived a woman named Pascadozzia. One day Pascadozzia saw a beautiful parsley plant in the garden of her neighbor, the ogress. Oh, how she longed for the parsley! So great was her longing that she crept into the garden and stole some. This went on for days, until one day, the ogress caught her.

"Thief!" exclaimed the ogress. "Now you must pay."

Pascadozzia tried to make excuses. But the ogress shrugged her shoulders and said, "Words are but wind. You must die OR give me your first child."

Poor Pascadozzia agreed to give the ogress her child.

Some months later Pascadozzia gave birth to a baby girl. She named her Parsley, for she was born with a sprig of parsley on her chest. When Parsley was 7 years old, the ogress snatched her away. She locked the girl in a tall tower. Whenever the ogress wanted to see Parsley, she climbed up the girl's long hair.

Many years later a prince appeared. He saw Parsley's hair hanging from the tower window. He called out. When their eyes met, the prince and Parsley fell instantly in love.

The prince wanted to climb up. But the visit had to be kept secret. So Parsley slipped the ogress poppy juice. The juice made the ogress fall into a deep sleep.

The next morning, as the prince climbed down Parsley's hair, a gossipy friend of the ogress saw him.

She told the ogress, who replied, "Thank you. But do not fear. It's impossible for Parsley to escape. I have laid a spell upon her. Unless she's holding the three gallnuts that are hidden above the kitchen rafters, the spell cannot be broken."

Luckily Parsley overheard the ogress. That night, when the prince came, she had him climb the rafters and get the gallnuts. Then, holding the gallnuts in her hand, she and the prince climbed down a rope ladder and escaped.

The ogress' friend saw them. She hollered and woke the ogress, who quickly chased after Parsley and the prince.

Parsley, knowing the gallnuts were magical, threw one at the ground. It turned into a Corsican bulldog! The beast chomped its jaws and leapt at the ogress. But the cunning ogress pulled out a piece of bread and gave it to the dog, which made the dog's anger disappear.

Parsley threw the second gallnut. It turned into a lion! The beast shook its mane and opened its jaws wide.

But the ogress stripped off the skin of a donkey that was grazing nearby. Wearing the skin, she charged the lion. The lion, thinking the ogress was an angry donkey, became frightened and ran away.

Parsley looked into her hand. She had one gallnut left. She threw it, and it turned into a wolf! Seeing the ogress in the donkey skin, the hungry wolf pounced. In a blink, it ate her.

At last Parsley and the prince were free of the ogress. They married and lived happily ever after.

Glossary

Corsican bulldog–a bulldog with large jaws that comes from the Italian island of Corsica

culture–a people's way of life, ideas, art, customs, and traditions

gallnut–an abnormal growth of plant tissue (often found on oak trees) that looks like a nut

ogress–a female monster or giant that eats people; the male version is called an ogre

proclamation–an official announcement

rapunzel–a kind of flowering plant that has a white root you can eat; also known as rampion

sorceress–a woman with magical powers

spurn–to turn away or reject

Critical Thinking Using the Common Core

Look at the illustrations for *Rapunzel*. What details show you that the story takes place in Germany? (Key Ideas and Details)

How do Juan's actions contribute to the sequence of events in *Clotilde*? (Craft and Structure)

What does the ogress in *Petrosinella* mean when she says, "Words are but wind?" (Integration of Knowledge and Ideas)

Writing Prompts

1) Write your own version of *Petrosinella* set in modern times. What could you use instead of gallnuts? What creatures could you write about instead of a Corsican bulldog, a lion, and a wolf?

2) Write a "reader's theater" script for one of the stories in this book.

Read More

Isadora, Rachel, retold and illustrated by. *Rapunzel / Written by the Brothers Grimm.* New York: G. P. Putnam's Sons, 2008.

Peters, Stephanie, retold by. *Rapunzel: The Graphic Novel.* Graphic Spin. Minneapolis: Stone Arch Books, 2009.

Sage, Alison. *Rapunzel: Based on the Original Story by the Brothers Grimm.* Chicago: Albert Whitman, 2011.

Internet Sites

FactHound offers a safe, fun way to find Internet sites related to this book. All of the sites on FactHound have been researched by our staff.

Here's all you do:

Visit *www.facthound.com*

Type in this code: 9781479554362

Thanks to our advisers for their expertise and advice:

Maria Tatar, PhD, Chair, Program in Folklore & Mythology
John L. Loeb Professor of Germanic Languages & Literatures and Folklore & Mythology
Harvard University

Terry Flaherty, PhD, Professor of English
Minnesota State University, Mankato

Editor: Jill Kalz
Designer: Ashlee Suker
Art Director: Nathan Gassman
Production Specialist: Katy LaVigne
The illustrations in this book were created digitally.

Picture Window Books are published by Capstone,
1710 Roe Crest Drive, North Mankato, Minnesota 56003
www.capstonepub.com

Copyright © 2015 by Picture Window Books, a Capstone imprint. All rights reserved. No part of this publication may be reproduced in whole or in part, or stored in a retrieval system, or transmitted in any form or by any means, electronic, mechanical, photocopying, recording, or otherwise, without written permission of the publisher.

Library of Congress Cataloging-in-Publication Data
Meister, Cari, author.
Rapunzel stories around the world : 3 beloved tales / by Cari Meister.
pages cm. – (Nonfiction picture books. Multicultural fairy tales)
Summary: Retells the classic German tale of Rapunzel in the tower, along with the similar tales of Clotilde from the Philippines, and Petrosinella from Italy.
Includes bibliographical references.
ISBN 978-1-4795-5436-2 (library binding)
ISBN 978-1-4795-5452-2 (paperback)
ISBN 978-1-4795-5444-7 (paper over board)
ISBN 978-1-4795-5460-7 (eBook PDF)
1. Fairy tales. 2. Folklore–Germany. [1. Fairy tales. 2. Folklore.]
I. Rapunzel. English. II. Title.
PZ8.M5183Rap 2015
398.2–dc23 2014006637

Look for all the books in the series:

Printed in the United States 5914